Introductio

Llandrindod Wells, the county town of Powys
Edwardian buildings, as well as formal and i
network of recently improved footpaths surrour
local beauty spots at Cefnllys and Alpine Bridge, une woodlands to the north
of the town, the remains of the largest Roman Fort in Wales (at Castell Collen)
and across the hill to the nearby village of Howey.

Walking routes also connect Llandrindod Wells with some of the other
towns and villages in the area. Builth Wells, the home of the Royal Welsh
Agricultural Show, can be reached by a varied 10 mile walk that includes the
Carneddau hills and a Wye-side path. The town provides a choice between
easy riverside walking and a chance to explore the hills to the south.

Another route from Llandrindod Wells leads to Newbridge-on-Wye, where
a number of circular routes can be explored, including those making use of
the Wye Valley Walk for part of the way. From Newbridge-on-Wye you can
take a route over the hills to the spectacular Elan Valley (reservoirs and nature
conservation area), passing through National Trust land on the way.

A network of train, bus and Post Bus services, centring on Llandrindod
Wells, connect the places mentioned in this guide and also make linear
walks an option. A walk can be taken over the hill from Nantmel to historic
Abbey Cwmhir, with a return to Llandrindod Wells by Post Bus. A route
from Llandegley Village leads past the striking outcroppings at Llandegley
Rocks and over the hills to Llandrindod Wells. Penybont Village, on route to
Llandegley, provides the opportunity to walk around common land with hill
views and visit a traditional village shop.

Each walk includes a map and directions, enabling the route to the
followed without difficulty. Footpaths and bridlepaths are frequently
waymarked, particularly near the towns. When crossing open access land
(where a number of parallel paths can exist) a suggested route is included.
Details of specific public transport operators are included in the information
for individual walks, when relevant. The Powys Travel Guide, available free
from Tourist Information Centres, gives comprehensive details of public
transport in the area.

The use of walking boots and suitable clothing for walks contained in this
guide is recommended. Walkers are also advised to check weather forecasts,
particularly if following upland paths (weather information for the next
five days is available from www.bbc.co.uk/wales/weather) or from Tourist
Information Centres (Llandrindod Wells 01597 822600, Builth Wells 01982
553307 or Rhayader 01597 810591). The location of each walk and its starting
point is shown on and inside the back cover, with estimated walking times.
Allow extra time if exploring places of interest on the route. Please follow the
country code and – enjoy your walking!

LLANDRINDOD WELLS' GREEN SPACES

DESCRIPTION An attractive walk of some 4 miles, via Temple Gardens, Memorial Gardens and County Hall grounds to Llandrindod Wells Lake and the adjacent Woodland Walk. The route then leads across a grassy area and by quiet road and lane to a footpath leading to Rock Park, where an attractive riverside walk is followed above the Ithon. can be muddy in places.Allow about 2 hours.

START Railway Station, Car Park and Bus stops in central Llandrindod Wells. SO 059614.

PUBLIC TRANSPORT Llandrindod Wells – trains, plus several bus services. (See Powys Travel Guide, available free from Tourist Information Centres in Powys, for details).

I From the Railway Station (Booking Office side), head RIGHT past Boots and turn RIGHT into Middleton Street. Cross the junction at the end of Middleton Street to Temple Gardens (see Information Board near entrance to the gardens). Bear LEFT through the gardens towards the Metropole Hotel. Go over the zebra crossing on the left, follow the pavement to the right and then turn LEFT into Memorial Gardens (see Information Board near entrance to the gardens). Go past the Museum (*recently renovated and well worth a visit*) and over a footbridge. Turn RIGHT on reaching the road. On reaching the junction, cross and follow the driveway up towards County Hall. Go past the statue of Gaea, on the right, and take the footpath on the right. Follow this to the road and then turn LEFT. *This section of the route passes trees planted in 1946 to commemorate Brecon and Radnor's contribution to the Red Cross Agriculture Fund. The remains of St. Maelog's Chapel – built in the late 12th century and demolished in the 16th – can also be seen on the left.* Continue around the Lake – *created in 1872-3 on the site of a former peat bog* – passing metal gates on the left.

2 On reaching a waymarked kissing gate and larger gate, turn LEFT (notice the information board on the right, which gives details of what may be seen on the woodland walk). Follow the track and then path ahead until reaching a white arrow waymark sign on the right. Turn RIGHT here and follow the path through the woodland. At a junction of paths, continue AHEAD, now on a gravelled section. On reaching the road, turn LEFT and follow the pavement around the Lake, *to reach the Lakeside Cafe, shop and other facilities.*

3 Take the path leading up the bank near the carving of a 'Llandoddie' ('mythological' figure associated with the Lake area) onto the Common. Cross the grass and follow a path through trees. Turn LEFT and cross another area of grass to pass through the commemorative trees – *planted to mark the coronation of George VI in 1936* – and head RIGHT down to the Ridgebourne shops. Cross the road and take the no-through lane down the left side of the Grosvenor Stores (bakery).

4 Pass under the Railway Bridge and shortly thereafter bear HALF RIGHT on a waymarked footpath. Take the left fork and follow the path – *the open area to right is the site of a Roman practice ground* – to Rock Park. Turn LEFT on the tarmac path and LEFT again. Continue AHEAD to join a waymarked path following the site of a Roman Road. Pass to the left of the Bowling Club. At the next junction, continue AHEAD following the waymark sign. Bypass the next waymark post and descend to a footbridge and kissing gate. Follow the Ithon along the edge of the field. The stepping stones shown on the map are not currently present but it is planned to restore these, hopefully in 2007. At the end of the field, retrace your steps to and through the kissing gate and over the footbridge.

5 Follow the railings on the left to the steps on the left. Turn LEFT to follow a path above the River Ithon. Follow a further three waymark posts and bear LEFT onto a path that leads above a stream to the Rock Park

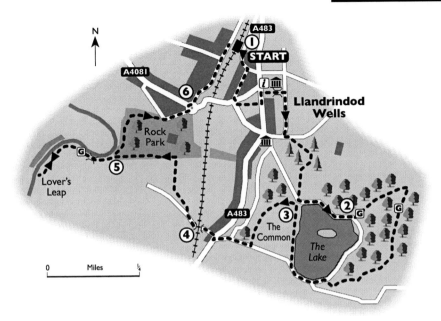

Visitor Centre. Head LEFT around the building and cross the car park area. Continue AHEAD, following the waymark post. Follow wooden railings down to the left, past the Chalybeate Spring. Head LEFT and, at a junction of paths, take the second from the right. Head up towards the Park entrance.

6 Cross the road to the left, passing the front of Y Gwalia – *the former Radnorshire Council headquarters*. Continue AHEAD along the High Street (*some of the buildings to the left have recently been renovated, as part of the High Street improvement project*) to reach the Magistrates Court and Police Station (opposite the Railway Station). The road on the left, immediately after the Police Station, leads to the **Llanerch Inn**, an 18th century coaching inn.

Llandoddie

CASTELL COLLEN, LLANFIHANGEL HELYGEN & LLANYRE

DESCRIPTION A 6½ mile walk, with attractive views throughout. The route goes from Llandrindod Wells town centre by cycle path/footpath, quiet road and lane to Castell Collen Roman fort. The walk then follows a footpath route to the church at Llanfihangel Helygen, before following lane and footpath to Llanyre, where a pub lunch is available. From here, the cycling/walking route can be followed back to Llandrindod Wells, or a bus caught from Llanyre. Allow about 3¾ hours for the walk.

START Railway Station/bus stops/car park in central Llandrindod Wells. SO 059614.

PUBLIC TRANSPORT Llandrindod Wells is on the Heart of Wales line and has several bus services, all of which stop near the Railway Station (See Powys Travel Guide, available from Tourist Information Centres in Powys, for general information). Llanyre is on the Crossgates bus route between Llandrindod Wells and Rhayader (01597 85200). There is also a weekday Post Bus service (01597 822925).

I From the Railway Station (Police Station side), cross the road to the Magistrate's Court. Follow Dyffryn Road down the left side of this building (signposted for the Sports Centre). Pass the entrance to the High School and turn RIGHT onto a waymarked Cycling/Walking path. Follow this until reaching the entrance to a housing estate. Continue AHEAD on Holcombe Avenue, and then turn RIGHT into Holcombe Drive. At the t-junction, turn LEFT and follow the road down to the junction with the main road.

2 Join the cycle/walking route on the right and follow this across the Ithon Bridge. Follow the path to the RIGHT and go up steps to a stile. Head to the right of the enclosure fence and then bear HALF LEFT to reach a stile onto a lane. Turn RIGHT in the lane and follow this past 'Cwm' on the left. When the road bends to the right, follow this to the house at the end of the track. Go past the house, through a gate and over a stile to reach Castell Collen – *the site of a large Roman Fort, occupied between the 1st and 4th centuries AD.*

3 When ready, retrace your steps past the house and along the lane, until reaching the bend to the left. Cross the stile on the right and take the left hand fork in the footpath. Head HALF LEFT across the field, to cross a stile into a wooded area. Cross a small stream and maintain your direction out of the trees and across two fields, connected by a gate. Cross the second field to a stile and then follow the right hand boundary of a third field to reach a gate onto a road.

4 Turn RIGHT and follow the road for a short way, to a waymarked gate on the left (just before Castell-Gwynt, on the right). Cross the field, passing just to the left of a pile of stones, to a gate. Continue along the right hand side of the field and then head SLIGHTLY TO THE LEFT to reach a stile. Cross the next field, keeping to the left of the wooded area. Follow the fenceline on the right to reach a stile into the grounds of St Michael in the Willows church – *which has box pews, an 11th century font and a 14th century roof.*

5 When ready, leave the church grounds and turn LEFT along the lane (passing benches on the left that provide a scenic place to take a break). Cross Pentre Bach Bridge. Turn RIGHT at the junction with a smaller lane, opposite Bryn-bedwen. Continue along the lane, until reaching the end of the third field on the left. Pass through a gate on the left and follow the track through a waymarked gate and across a narrow field. At the next waymarked gate, head HALF LEFT to a stile – *traditional hedgelaying has taken place here.* Continue AHEAD over the next two stiles and then head SLIGHTLY LEFT to a further stile. Cross the stile and a small stream. Climb the bank to a stile onto a track.

6 Turn LEFT and follow the track to the junction with the road through Llanyre. Turn RIGHT and follow the road through the village to reach the **Gold Bell Inn** on the right – *a 17th Century inn, at which pub lunches are available.* The route leads past Llanyre Hall (by a road junction on the left) and the Pritchard Recreation Ground – *a wooded area containing a short walk, also on the left.*

Ithon Bridge, cross a stile on the right and follow the footpath HALF LEFT across two fields, connected a gate, and cross a final stile to rejoin the main road. Cross with care and head RIGHT along the pavement. On reaching the junction with Dyffryn Road (on the left) turn LEFT and follow the road back past the High School to the Magistrates Court. *If you wish to shorten the walk, a bus can be caught back from Llanyre – see public transport information in the start of walk details.*

Llanfihangel-helygen

Bryn bedwen

Llanyre

Castell Collen Roman Fort

Llanyre Bridge

A4081

Afon leithon

N

Llandrindod Wells

START · A483

0   Miles   ½

7 When ready to leave Llanyre, retrace your steps to the turning by Llanyre Hall. Turn RIGHT here and follow the lane to the junction with the main road. Join the cycle/walking route on the left and follow this towards Llandrindod Wells. Shortly after crossing the

5

TWO BRIDGES WALK

DESCRIPTION An 8 mile walk. Starting from the (Victorian) man-made Llandrindod Lake, this route climbs through broadleaved woodland and hill pastures to a viewpoint, before descending to historic Cefnllys, the site of a medieval town, of which only the church now remains. The riverside location is overlooked by a hill that was the site of a Marcher Castle. Nearby is Bailey Einon Woodland Nature Reserve, from which the walk runs through woods and fields to Alpine Bridge, where the Ithon cuts through a small gorge. The return journey to the Lake also follows a mixture of woodland and hill paths, providing further good views of the area. Allow about 5 hours for the walk.

START Llandrindod Wells Lake. SO 063606.

PUBLIC TRANSPORT Llandrindod Wells – trains, plus several bus services. (See Powys Travel Guide, available free from TICs in Powys, for general information).

I From the Lakeside tourist facilities, follow the pavement around the Lake in a clockwise direction until reaching a gate and kissing gate on the left, by an information board. Pass through and follow the waymarked track, through broadleaved woodland. After passing an open grassy section, look out for two waymark posts. Ignore the first (with the white arrow) and head for the second (yellow arrow). Follow the path along the side of the field until reaching a further waymark post, just before a stile. Do not cross the stile, but turn RIGHT and head up the bank to turn HALF LEFT on one of several paths. Follow this for a while, then bear RIGHT and head up out of the woodland. Continue AHEAD towards a patch of gorse. Cross the stile and skirt the gorse, then continue uphill towards the next fence. Continue AHEAD over the next three fields, connected by stiles. Cross the stile into the fourth field and continue up to the trig point and cairns.

2 Continue AHEAD to a stile onto the lane and turn LEFT. Descend towards Llanoley until reaching a waymarked track on the left (opposite a waymark post on the right). Go through a gate on the left and past Upper Llanoley. Go through a footgate and continue along the waymarked track, descending gradually towards Cefnllys. Pass through a gate onto the lane; follow this to the RIGHT for a short way, until reaching the entrance gate to the church area. *Only the church now remains of the medieval village, although the uneven ground indicates the location of previous dwellings – the population declined in the 1800s. The site of the castle is well worth climbing for the views. For the easiest ascent, cross the field from the main entrance to the church, go through and gate and head left along the track, to reach the lower north end of the hill.* Visit this area and return to the lane when ready to go on.

3 Pass through the footgate on the right into the woodland nature reserve and follow the boardwalk path (information board near the entrance provides details concerning the site). Pass through a footgate at the far end – there are sturdy handrails on the steeper sections of the path beyond this point. Continue along the woodland path and then head up a clear path to a stile. Continue HALF LEFT to reach a waymark post. Head RIGHT and cross a stile. Follow the right boundary of the field to reach another stile and head towards the house lower down the field on the right.

4 Cross the track by means of stiles and continue AHEAD to a stile and shallow stream. Head HALF RIGHT to reach the next stile and then continue AHEAD towards the wooded area. Cross a stile and take a path (faint for the first few yards) that runs slightly to the left for a short way and then turns half right up the bank. Leave the wood via a gate on the left and then proceed up the bank towards a waymark post. Turn RIGHT and continue AHEAD past a marker post to the left hand of two gates. Continue AHEAD, in line with farm buildings now visible on the other side of the river. On reaching the riverbank, by a waymark post, turn LEFT and follow the track through another wooded area and up towards a farm. On reaching the farm track, pass through a gate, turn RIGHT and pass through another gate on the right. The path leads down to Alpine Bridge, with its views of the Ithon.

5 Retrace your steps to Cefnllys. Just before leaving the Nature Reserve, turn RIGHT through a footgate. Follow the footpath up the hill, keeping to the left of lower ground on the right and cross a stile onto the lane. Turn RIGHT and follow the lane to a t-junction. Continue round to the left at this point, until reaching Bailey Einon farm, on the right. Pass through a gate onto the footpath opposite the farm and follow this up the left side of the first two fields, connected by stiles. On reaching the waymark post at the beginning of the third field, cross the stile, head RIGHT to a gap in the fence and then cross a stile and turn LEFT on a track.

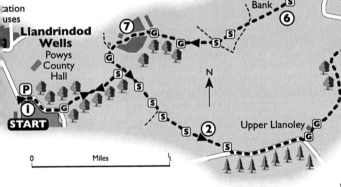

stream on the left. On reaching a large rock, head LEFT to a kissing gate and follow a fenced path to the road.

6 On reaching a waymark post on the left, bear HALF LEFT across open ground towards another waymark post visible near trees ahead. Cross a track and head HALF LEFT towards conifers. Cross a stile into this small plantation and follow the path to a stile on the right. Head across the field towards a waymark post by an area of gorse. Follow the path down between gorse bushes for a short way and go through a footgate into a wooded area. Follow the path down the right hand side of the valley, above a

7 Cross the road and follow the fenced path. On reaching a second road, cross and turn RIGHT to reach a third section of the fenced path on the left. Follow the path for a few yards, and then turn RIGHT and almost immediately LEFT. Continue ahead to a waymark post. Bear HALF LEFT at this point, to reach a stile back into the woodland adjacent to Llandrindod Lake. Retrace your steps alongside the field and continue AHEAD to return to the lakeside road.

LLANDRINDOD WELLS WOODLAND CIRCULAR

DESCRIPTION A 5 mile walk starting from Llandrindod Lake and passing through attractive areas of woodland and fields with hill views, plus the site of a former quarry (now an attractive 'wetland' setting). Allow about 3 hours for the walk.
START Llandrindod Lake. SO 063606.
PUBLIC TRANSPORT Llandrindod Wells – trains plus several bus services (See Powys Travel Guide, available free from Tourist Information Centres in Powys, for details).

I From the Lakeside tourist facilities, follow the road around the lake in a clockwise direction until reaching the gate and kissing gate on the left next to an information board. Pass through and follow the track up into deciduous woodland. Cross a grassy area and follow the waymark post with a yellow arrow (ignore the waymark post just before this, with white arrow). Follow the path along the side of a field to a stile by a waymark post. Cross the stile and head HALF LEFT across the field to another waymark post. Bear RIGHT here and pass through a kissing gate. Take the left fork in the path and follow this to a kissing-gate onto a lane.

2 Turn RIGHT in the lane and follow this to junction with a minor road. Cross the road and take the waymarked lane opposite. At the end of the lane, descend waymarked steps on the left into a wooded area. Cross the footbridge over Arlais Brook and head up the bank to a stile. Head up the field, past a telegraph pole – *there are excellent 360 degree views from the top of the field.* Cross a stile on the right and keep to the left of the field. Bear HALF LEFT on reaching the waymark post by the hedge on the left. Cross a stile to the left of a gate and continue AHEAD between fences to reach a gate onto a lane.

3 Turn LEFT on the lane, passing houses to both sides. Look out for a waymark post on the right and follow the footpath RIGHT across open ground towards a small rock outcropping. At another waymark post, bear HALF RIGHT, still across open ground. *The quarry – on the right – is fenced off, as a danger area, but provides attractive views of what appears to be now a wetland area.* Keep to the left of the stream to reach a waymarked stile. Head along the right hand side of the field. Follow the path HALF RIGHT, and then bear LEFT to reach a waymarked stile. Cross and head along the field, then bear RIGHT to reach a stile on the left, near the entrance to Noyadd.

4 Pass to the left of the entrance and then follow the track AHEAD, passing below Noyadd. Go LEFT at the fork in the track. At a bend to the right in the track, pass through a waymarked gate AHEAD and follow the track, bearing HALF RIGHT at the next waymark post. Continue AHEAD to a waymarked gate. Take the left fork and head HALF LEFT at next waymark post. Go through a waymarked footgate and into a woodland area. Follow the path AHEAD and bear HALF RIGHT at the next waymark post. Cross a small stream and head HALF RIGHT at the next waymark post.

5 Pass through a footgate and follow an old track along the left hand side of a field (divert RIGHT around boggy section). Ignore the stile on the left and continue AHEAD through a waymarked gate and along the left hand edge of the next two fields, connected by gates. Cross a farm access track and continue AHEAD to another gate. Follow the track, now along the right hand side of two fields, again connected by gates. Continue AHEAD, keeping to the left of track where this route is shared with a stream. Go LEFT at two junctions of track to reach a gate onto a lane.

6 Turn RIGHT in the lane and follow the lane round to the right. Look out for a

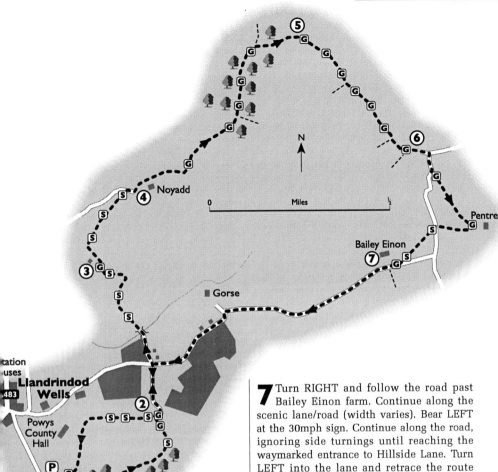

7 Turn RIGHT and follow the road past Bailey Einon farm. Continue along the scenic lane/road (width varies). Bear LEFT at the 30mph sign. Continue along the road, ignoring side turnings until reaching the waymarked entrance to Hillside Lane. Turn LEFT into the lane and retrace the route through the kissing gate on the left at the end of the lane. Bear RIGHT to return to the first waymark post and then bear RIGHT again to cross a stile. Follow a clear path across a field to a second stile and continue along the wooded path to a third stile. Cross and take the wooden steps on the left. Turn RIGHT at the top and follow the path through attractive woodland. On coming in sight of a house, bear RIGHT, passing to the right of an oak tree, and take the left fork in the path. *Powys County Council Headquarters is visible on the right and the Lake can be seen ahead.* Continue along the path, which now descends towards the Lake and passes through a final footgate. Turn RIGHT to return to the Lakeside tourist facilities.

waymarked footgate on the left. Go through and head HALF RIGHT across the field to an open gateway – *notice the view of Castle Bank, Cefnllys, beyond the house ahead.* Continue along the left hand side of the next field to a footgate onto a track. Turn RIGHT and follow the track to a lane. Cross the lane and the stile opposite and head HALF LEFT across the field towards the trees. Cross a stile and follow the path through the trees to a footgate onto the road.

LLANDRINDOD HILL

To station & buses

Llandrindod Wells

A483

Powys County Hall

START

The Lake

Llandrindod Hall

Ty Gwyn Bach

Broomy Hill

golf course

DESCRIPTION A 7 mile walk, climbing from Llandrindod Wells Lake, this route passes the old parish church and follows upland pastures (and the local golf course) to the scenic hills and valleys east of Llandrindod Wells. Upland pastures and open access land with further excellent views are followed to reach Llanoley, from where the route returns to the lake via a local viewpoint.

START Llandrindod Wells Lake. SO 063606.

PUBLIC TRANSPORT Buses and trains in Llandrindod Wells centre (see Powys Travel Guide, available free from Tourist Information Centres in Powys, for details).

I From the Lakeside tourist facilities, follow the pavement around the Lake in a clockwise direction. Ignore the bridlepath sign on the left (by a kissing gate and larger gate) and continue to a footpath sign, also on the left. Follow the path, which is gravelled for the first section, into the woodland area. Follow the path up and to the right to reach a junction with another path, just after an information board on the left. Continue AHEAD for a short way, pass through a footgate and bear RIGHT towards the church.

2 Go through a waymarked gate onto the road. Cross with care and cross the left side of the churchyard by means of gates – *the church is originally 13th Century, but was rebuilt in 1894.* Follow the churchyard wall round to the right, to reach a footgate and steps in the corner of the field. Descend and turn LEFT on the track. Pass through a gate and follow the track round to the right. Go through the next gateway and take the left fork in the track, alongside a fence on the left. When the fence turns uphill, follow a track that heads slightly to the left and climbs steadily through bracken. Pass through a gate and continue AHEAD along the track, passing between two sheep feeders. Just before reaching a next gate, head HALF

LEFT (by a waymark post) and go uphill towards another stile in the fence ahead.

3 Cross the field to another stile and follow the path to a waymark post. Turn LEFT here and head up the left hand side of the field to a waymarked stile. Cross and continue up the field to a waymarked footgate onto the golf course. Keep close to the fence on the right and follow the path around the edge of the golf course (*keep an eye for golf balls!*). Ignore stiles without waymarking (these appear to give golfers access to adjacent fields). Eventually, cross a waymarked stile on the right and head to the far left corner of the field to reach a waymarked gate, next to a stone wall. Pass through and follow the wall along the right hand side of the field to reach another waymarked gate. Pass through and head HALF LEFT across the field, aiming just to the left of a line of trees to reach a stile (part hidden by the trees). Cross and continue HALF LEFT to reach a stile onto a lane.

4 Turn LEFT in the lane and continue to a T-junction. Turn RIGHT and descend towards the house (Carregwiber). Pass to the right of the house, following the footpath waymark signs. Continue along the track, passing to the left of a small lake. Remain on the track over two cattlegrids. On coming in sight of a farmhouse (Lower

Upper Llanoley, Lower Llanoley

⑦

Bank House — Pen-rhiw Frank

G – – G ▼

G

Carreg-wiber Bank — Bwlchyfedwen

G

N ↑

④

Ⓢ Ⓢ

■ Carregwiber

0   Miles   ½

⑥ G

G

G

G

⑤ G   Gilwern Hill
G

Gilwern), bear LEFT on a track, go through a gate and continue up the track. Climb gradually and follow the track round to the right, taking the left fork at the junction in tracks.

5 Pass through a gate and continue AHEAD on more level ground. Follow the track around to the left (passing Upper Gilwern on the right). Keep to the left side of a line of old fencing to reach a wider track now visible ahead. Turn left on the wider track. Follow

this uphill for a short way and then around to the left. Pass through two gates and continue on across the hillside, keeping to the left of the fenceline (the track leads only to a barn). Aim towards the more distant of two cairns (on a hill top slightly to the right), passing through a gate on the way – after this follow a clear track and then continue ahead across open ground.

6 Pass through a gate to the left of the cairn and cross the open ground towards a track by an area of trees. Turn LEFT and pass through a gate. Keep to the left of the sunken track (this has wet patches) and rejoin the main route just before the next gate. Continue along the track, passing through a number of footgates and passing a cottage on the right. Follow the track down to Llanoley, bearing RIGHT on the bridlepath rather than following a footpath to the left. Pass through a footgate and continue along the track to join the end of a lane.

7 Climb the hill, passing Lower and Upper Llanoley on the right. Take the second stile on the right. Head up the bank to the trig point and cairns. From here, follow a clear path ahead over three stiles. Follow a path that runs just to the left of a tree. Skirt gorse bushes to reach another stile. Continue downhill towards the woodland, taking the right fork in the path.

8 On entering the woodland, bear HALF LEFT on one of several paths. Soon, head to the RIGHT, through a gap in the trees to a waymark post near a fence. Turn LEFT and follow the waymarked path and then track to reach the Lake. Turn RIGHT to reach the Lakeside tourist facilities.

LLANDRINDOD WELLS TO CROSSGATES

DESCRIPTION A walk of some 5½ miles. This route visits a small nature reserve, then heads up through deciduous woodland to a hilltop walk with excellent views, before descending by footpath and track to the scenic Ithon valley. From here, footpaths, tracks and lane are followed through fields and woods, including riverside sections, to reach Crossgates (from where bus and train services are available to return to Llandrindod Wells). Allow about 3 hours.

START Tourist Information Centre, Fiveways, Llandrindod Wells. SO 060619.

PUBLIC TRANSPORT *Crossgates* is on the bus route to Llandrindod Wells (three services currently operate via the bus stop on the road to Llandrindod Wells). *Penybont Station* is close to the end of the route. There is also a weekday afternoon Post Bus service operating via Penybont and Crossgates. (See Powys Travel Guide, available free from Tourist Information Centres in Powys, for general information).

1 From outside the Tourist Information Centre, head RIGHT (passing Coleg Powys on the left and the entrance to County Hall on the right). Continue along the road past the Welsh Assembly building and the school. Cross over 'Woodlands' and 'Hillside Lane', both on the right. At the end of the uphill section (before the housing estate and the Post Box on the right) turn RIGHT through a foot-entrance to the right of a metal gate. Follow the tarmac path along the right-hand-side of Gorse Farm Nature Reserve (beyond the wooden railings on the left). Cross the footbridge and ascend the steps, then bear LEFT to reach a Radnorshire Wildlife Trust information board about the reserve. When ready, bear RIGHT along the rest of the path to a road.

2 Bear LEFT, RIGHT and then LEFT again to reach a T-junction. Turn RIGHT at the T-junction. Look out for a waymark post on the left and follow the footpath between fences to reach a footgate into a field. Follow the path across the field, passing to the right of a rock and continue AHEAD, up through a wooded area, above a stream on the right. Pass through a footgate and follow a short path up through gorse bushes. Continue AHEAD across the field and cross a stile into a forestry plantation. After a short distance, bear LEFT on a path that cuts diagonally through the small plantation to a stile.

3 Continue AHEAD in the same direction until reaching a track. Bear LEFT along the track (which provides a range of hill views to the left) until reaching a stile on the left, by a footgate. Cross and descend the field towards another stile onto the road. Turn RIGHT and follow the scenic road route until reaching Bailey Einon farm on the left. Just after the farm, turn LEFT through a footgate into a small wood. Follow the path through the wood to a stile. Bear HALF LEFT across the field to another stile, giving on to a lane. Cross the lane and take the waymarked track opposite. Follow the track between farm buildings and round to the left.

4 Pass through a gate and continue along the track. At the end of the track, pass through a gate and head along the right hand side of a field to an open gateway. Descend the hill – *excellent views ahead at this point* – towards a house. Cross the track by means of stiles and continue AHEAD to a stile and shallow stream. Head HALF RIGHT to reach the next stile and then continue AHEAD towards the wooded area. Cross a stile into the wood and follow a track (faint at first) which leads half left for a short way, then bends round to the right. Follow this to the top of the wood and exit via a gate on the left.

5 Continue up the field to a waymark post and turn RIGHT. Continue ahead along the track, passing another way-

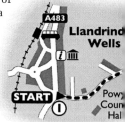

12

mark post to reach two gates. Pass through the left hand gate and head down the field to the bank of the River Ithon. Turn LEFT on reaching a waymark post and follow the track through a gate and into a wooded area. Continue along the track, climbing to a gate near a farmhouse. Bear RIGHT on the track (Alpine Bridge – *where the Ithon flows through a small gorge* – can be reached via a waymarked footgate on the right. After visiting this, return to the main route and turn right) and continue AHEAD through a gate. Follow the track along the left hand side of a field to a further gate. Pass through and continue along the right hand side of the next field to a further gateway by an old stile.

6 Immediately after the gateway, turn RIGHT and follow the right hand edge of the fields to the Ithon. Turn LEFT and follow the river bank along to a stile to the right of a gate. Head up a track, which is joined by another track from the left. Look out for a waymark post on a bank to the right. Turn RIGHT at the waymark post and head down the right hand side of the field – *excellent views also at this point* – to a stile. Cross and continue AHEAD, descending to the right of a farm building.

7 Continue HALF LEFT along the field to a stile. Follow the path up wooden steps and cross a stile onto the roadside. Turn RIGHT and cross the Ithon Bridge. Continue along the main road for a short way, passing through a lay-by, to take the second lane on the

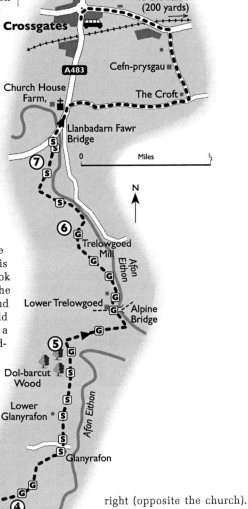

right (opposite the church). Follow the lane to a T-junction and then turn LEFT. Follow the lane down to the junction with the Crossgates to Penybont Road. To reach the Railway Station, turn RIGHT and look out for the turning for the station (on the left – Penybont is a request stop, so signal as for a bus). To reach the bus stop at Crossgates, turn LEFT and LEFT again at the roundabout.

WALK 7
PENYBONT VILLAGE

DESCRIPTION Walks of either 4 or 8 miles. The longer route includes an attractive walk along a quiet lane with hedges and excellent views to the north. Penybont Village attractions include The Old Thomas Shop (shop, museum, cafe and gallery) and the **Severn Arms** (pub lunch and beer garden). Penybont Common was also the scene of a Quaker Revival in the 19th century. The Common (rough grazing with some patches of low-growing gorse) is open access land that gives a range of good views of the hills around. Allow about 2 or 4 hours for the walks, plus time to visit the village attractions.

START Either Penybont Railway Station. SO 099649) or Penybont Village. SO 116642.

PUBLIC TRANSPORT Penybont Railway Station (Heart of Wales Line – local information 01597 822053) or Sargeant's buses (Llandrindod Wells to Hereford service – 01544 230481) alighting in Penybont Village.

I If starting from Penybont Station (*8 mile option*), turn RIGHT on leaving the station. Take the first turning on the left and turn LEFT again at the T-junction. Follow the quiet lane (attractive hedges and views to the north) for about two miles to Penybont Village. At the junction with the main road, turn RIGHT and head down into the village.

The starting point for walkers joining the route in Penybont Village (*4 mile option*) – places to visit on the main road include the bridge over the River Ithon, The Old Thomas Shop and the **Severn Arms Hotel** (pub lunch available). To access the Common, take the Knighton road. Turn LEFT onto a waymarked footpath, crossing a stile on the left, just before a cattle grid.

2 The Common is now open access land but the following route gives good views of the land around. Follow the left hand boundary of the Common, which provides hill views and is bounded by attractive trees in places. At the further end of the Common, head back alongside the road and eventually cross to the southern half of the Common and bear HALF RIGHT. Keep to the higher ground on the way back towards the south. On approaching the main road, turn RIGHT onto a track that skirts a line of trees and return to Penybont Village.

3 To return to Penybont Station, follow the main road out of the village, passing the wooded grounds of the Hall (on the left) and turn LEFT onto the lane followed on the outward route. At the junction, turn RIGHT and head down towards the main road. Turn RIGHT again and follow the main road to the turning for the station, on the left. Penybont is a request stop, so signal as for a bus.

14

WALK 8

TOLL BRIDGE & WYE VALLEY

DESCRIPTION A 4½ mile walk, leading south from Newbridge-on-Wye, via road and scenic lane past the site of an old toll bridge to join the Wye Valley Walk. The route then leads through fields and includes a stretch of permissive footpath past the (Victorian) Jubilee Stone and along an additional section of the Wye, before returning to Newbridge-on-Wye. Allow about 2¾ hours.

START The Village Green, Newbridge-on-Wye. SO 016583.

PUBLIC TRANSPORT Newbridge-on-Wye is on the bus route to and from a number of local towns (see Powys Travel Guide, available free from Tourist Information Centres in Powys, for general information).

I From Newbridge Village Green, head LEFT on the A470 towards Builth Wells. Shortly before reaching the traffic lights, cross the road with care and join the cyclepath on the right. Follow the national cycleway into a minor road on the right. Follow this quiet, partially wooded, road to Brynwern Bridge.

2 Continue along the minor road, passing additional woodland and views of the hills towards Rhayader. Pass a Wye Valley Walk signpost pointing to the left and continue to another pointing to the right. Cross the stile on the right to join the Wye Valley Walk and head up the left side of the field. Cross a stile and follow the right hand boundary of the next field until reaching a waymark post in a gap on the right. Go through gap and head HALF LEFT to stile in the corner of field. Go through trees and straight AHEAD over next two stiles (with new hedge on left for part of way). Continue AHEAD down field to footbridge and stile. Follow the path up the bank to a waymark post. Head for the far left corner of the next field and pass through open gateway. Continue to left of next two fields, connected by open gateway.

3 Cross a further stile to gain a view of Estyn Wood, to which the Wye Valley Walk now leads. If the permissive path on the right is open, turn off onto this route. Cross the stile on the right and follow the tall waymark posts across the field, passing the (Victorian) Jubilee Stone and descending to the River Wye. Turn LEFT and follow the river bank. Later on, keep to the left of a fence. Eventually cross a stile to rejoin the Wye Valley Walk and cross another stile on the right into Estyn Wood. Follow the waymarked path up through the wood to a gate giving onto the Rhayader-Beulah road.

4 Turn RIGHT and follow the road back to Newbridge, passing Llysdinam

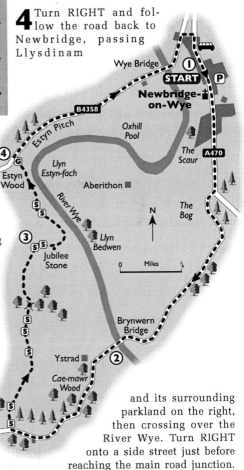

and its surrounding parkland on the right, then crossing over the River Wye. Turn RIGHT onto a side street just before reaching the main road junction. Turn RIGHT again onto the village street to return to the Village Green.

ABBEY CWMHIR

DESCRIPTION A 9½ mile walk, from the village of Nantmel to the historical site of Abbey Cwmhir. The route climbs from the village, to cross open land with scenic views, before descending on forestry tracks and footpath to Abbey Cwmhir. Once there, the site of the Abbey can be visited. A local cottage can be visited on specified days. The village has a pub and Post Office/shop. Allow about 5 or 6 hours for the walk.

START Railway Station, Car Park and Bus stops in central Llandrindod Wells. SO 059614.

PUBLIC TRANSPORT *Llandrindod Wells – Crossgates buses (01597 852000) operate to and from Nantmel (on route to Rhayader). As we go to press the last bus to Llandrindod Wells goes via Rhayader and Builth Wells.*

I Catch the bus to Nantmel, alighting at the War Memorial/Telephone Box. Take the lane that leads upwards past the village school and the church. Turn RIGHT on reaching the T-junction and continue to head uphill (there is a chance that Red Kites may be sighted over the hill to the left). Follow the lane over two cattle grids and then take the track on the left, which leads up and around the shoulder of the hill.

2 Continue on this track for some way. When it becomes faint (just after passing through a gate) keep close to the fence line on the right. Continue on the track once it becomes visible again, keeping to the main route and ignoring sheep tracks leading off to the left. Follow the track slightly down and to the right towards a group of conifers and ford a small stream.

3 After fording the stream, follow a faint track leading ahead and slightly to the left through the bracken. Go through a gate on the left – there is no visible track here, but turning RIGHT and following the fence line

on the right leads to a stile and gate into the forestry plantation ahead.

4 Follow the track ahead for a short way and then turn RIGHT on a forestry track (the shortcut footpath to the second junction below is overgrown at the time of writing). Continue to a junction of forestry tracks, heading round to the LEFT at this point. Descend, still on a forestry track, turning RIGHT at the second junction.

5 Just before reaching the third junction, take a path leading down to the left (this is a continuation of a path coming from the right). Descend, heading at first LEFT and then RIGHT, to a gate. Follow the track down the right hand side of the field to a second gate. Continue on the track, which bends right and then left to pass through another gate onto a road. Turn RIGHT and follow the road into Abbey Cwmhir village. *Abbey Cwmhir is the site of a Cistercian Abbey, founded circa 1176 and developed further in the 13th century. It was sacked during the course of Glyndwr's uprising. In 1644, during the Civil War, the site was attacked and captured by the Parliamentarians. The site is open to the public and contains a picnic site. The location is also associated with Llywelyn ap Gruffydd (the last native Prince of Wales), who is said to have been buried at the Abbey (see* **Walk 18***). The garden at Mill Cottage is in the National Gardens scheme (www. abbeycwmhir.co.uk, 01597 851935 for opening times). The village also contains a church (built in 1680), a Victorian Gothic Hall,* **The Happy Union** *pub and a Post Office/shop.*

6 Retrace the route back to Nantmel. Follow road back out of Abbey Cwmhir. Turn LEFT through gate and follow path back up to forestry track. Follow track back up to exit point from forestry. Head back across fields to re-cross small stream. Follow track up and to left and retrace route down to the lane. Turn RIGHT and follow lane down to Nantmel, turning LEFT at junction.

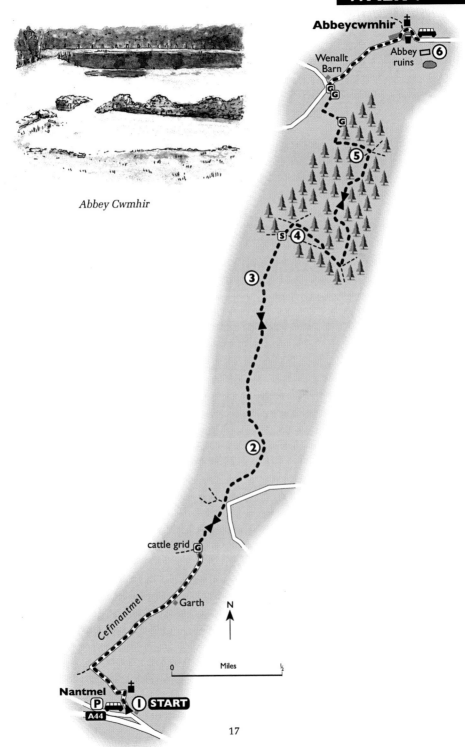

Abbeycwmhir

Wenallt
Barn

Abbey
ruins ⬜ ⑥

G G

G

⑤

S ④

③

②

N

cattle grid G

Cefnnantmel

Garth

Miles
0 ½

Nantmel
Ⓟ
A44 ① START

Abbey Cwmhir

CASTLE BANK CIRCULAR

DESCRIPTION A walk of either 6 or 10 miles, following a circular mainly upland route around open access land with a wide range of excellent views. The route passes the site of an old hill fort and includes some rough walking, but is never very far from a minor road. Allow 4 or 6 hours for the walk.

START Roadside parking by the Howey to Hundred House road, at SO 080569 OR bus stops at the Howey Village turn. SO 052588.

PUBLIC TRANSPORT Howey is on the main bus route between Llandrindod Wells and Builth Wells – there are various services, including TrawsCambria Brecon to Newtown. The walk is some two miles from the nearest bus route at Howey Village, but the consistently good views make it well worth the effort of following the minor road to get there (See Powys Travel Guide, available free from Tourist Information Centres in Powys, for details).

I *From the roadside parking place,* follow the road towards Howey, until just before the cattle grid. Turn LEFT to follow the boundary wall on the right around two small hills, *affording views towards the Carneddau Hills.*

From Howey Village turn bus stop, follow the road south to the Hundred House turning and then turn LEFT along this minor road (the course of an old Drover's Route from Newbridge-on-Wye to Kington, just over the border in England) for about two miles. After crossing a cattle grid, bear RIGHT to follow the boundary wall on the right around two small hills, affording views towards the Carneddau hills.

2 On completing the turn around the back of the second hill, follow a track that leads back toward the road. Just before reaching the road, turn RIGHT on another track that leads downhill, passing to the right of an enclosed area. Continue ahead and climb Castle Bank to the site of the old hill fort. As well as looking at the view from the summit, follow the circular path around the top of this long hill. When ready, head back down towards the road and follow this to the right and over the bridge to a lane.

3 Follow the unfenced lane until approaching the end of the open access area to the left. At this point, turn LEFT onto a path that runs alongside the field boundary, giving access to new views including of a previously hidden valley to the north. Continue alongside this boundary, using a mixture of tracks and sheep paths, until reaching a track by a gate signposted for Upper Gilwern. (The low-lying parts of this section can be wet and it may be necessary to temporarily divert to the left when passing through these).

4 Turn LEFT on the track and follow this back towards the road, passing a cottage on the way – this section of the route provides an excellent opportunity to look back over the ground covered during the circuit. On reaching the road, return to the parking place or turn RIGHT and retrace your steps to the Howey Village turn bus stop.

*To Ho\
& bus s\
1½ m*

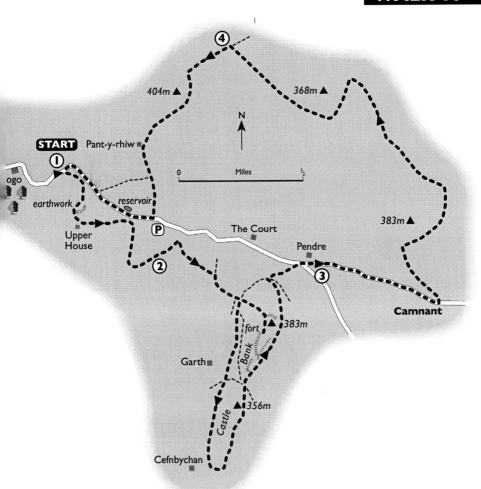

Castle Bank

LLANDEGLEY ROCKS & LITTLE HILL

DESCRIPTION A walk of 6½ miles, from the village of Llandegley to Llandrindod Wells. The route climbs from the village, to cross open land with striking rock outcroppings and scenic views, before joining a lane, bridlepath and footpath route to Llandrindod Wells. The latter part of the route passes a local viewpoint, above Llandrindod Wells Lake. Allow about 4 hours.

START Railway Station, Car Park and Bus stops in central Llandrindod Wells, SO 059614.

PUBLIC TRANSPORT Llandrindod Wells – Sargeant's buses operate to and from Llandegley, on route to Hereford (01544 230481).

I Alight from the bus on the main road (the bus is no longer able to go into the village but will stop at any safe place on the main road). Cross the main road with care and head for St Tecla's

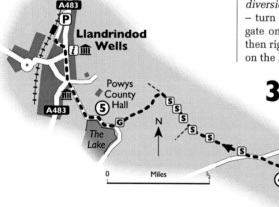

church – *part medieval, with a late medieval screen and ornate priest's door, the latter may have been brought from Abbey Cwmhir. The nave was rebuilt in 1876 and the tower in 1963.* Cross the churchyard by means of kissing gates to the right of the church and descend a flight of steps. Cross

the field to a stile and footbridge. Aim for the far left corner of the next field to join a path that leads uphill to a track. Turn LEFT on the track, continuing uphill. Pass through a gate and across a stone footbridge, passing a cottage on the right beyond trees. Continue on the track, which now crosses open hills. On meeting another track ascending from the right, turn LEFT and head to the left of the large rock outcropping ahead.

2 Cross a stile and head RIGHT to a gate. Continue through another gate and then pass to the right of a small conifer plantation to reach the next gate. Continue AHEAD, ignoring a path leading downhill to the left and pass to the right of another small area of conifers to reach an old gate (with a footpath waymark on the far side). Pass through the gate and turn LEFT. Follow the path through an area of gorse to another waymarked gate in the left corner of the enclosure. Turn RIGHT and cut across open ground to reach a track. The bridlepath, marked on the map as cutting diagonally across fields, has been abandoned in favour of following the track around the edges (*a County Council Rights of Way Officer has stated that this is the route used by most walkers and that an official diversion will be applied for in due course*) – turn LEFT and follow the track through a gate on the right, then round to the left and then right once more. Go past a group of trees on the left and through two gates.

3 Bear HALF LEFT, passing single conifers. Continue on the track, which soon bends to the right – *leading to a view of valley and lane* – and then left again. Follow the track along the brow of a hill and then down to a junction with the lane. Turn LEFT along the lane. When the lane bends to the left (next to a small area of conifers), take the track leading off to the right ('Road Closed to Vehicles' sign on main gate). Continue on this track, which is now clearly marked, going through several gates and passing to the left of a hilltop lake. Shortly after passing a cottage on the right, the track begins to descend towards a valley – look out for a waymark post on the left. Leave the track at this point to head down through a short area of bracken to a stile on the left. Cross, turn RIGHT and head towards a second stile and then skirt the boundary of the garden to reach a third stile. Turn LEFT along a path which is at first faint, but becomes clearer as it climbs and then bears right to join a lane.

4 Turn LEFT and follow the lane uphill for a short way, taking the second stile on the right. Head up the bank to the trig point and cairns. From here, follow a clear path ahead over three stiles. Follow a path that runs just to the left of a tree. Skirt gorse bushes to reach another stile. Continue downhill towards the woodland, taking the right fork in the path. On entering the woodland, bear HALF LEFT on one of several paths. Soon, head to the RIGHT, through a gap in the trees to a waymark post near a fence. Turn LEFT and follow the waymarked path and then track to reach the Lake.

5 Turn RIGHT and continue past the Lakeside tourist facilities and down to the junction near the Tourist Information Centre (on the left). Turn RIGHT and follow the road up past the Metropole Hotel to the zebra crossing. Cross and head RIGHT along the pavement. Turn LEFT and follow the road back down to the Railway Station area.

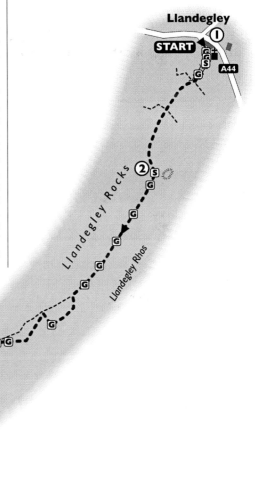

21

LLANDRINDOD WELLS TO BUILTH WELLS

DESCRIPTION A 10 mile walk, interesting not only for its views but for the variety of scenery that it includes – lakeside, woodland, upland sheep pastures, fields, country lane, open hills and finally a stretch of the river Wye Allow about 6 hours for the walk.. NB The permissive cycle route at the end of this walk is not available to walkers during Royal Welsh Show Week.
START Llandrindod Wells Lake. SO 063606.
PUBLIC TRANSPORT Llandrindod Wells, train and adjacent bus stops. Builth Wells, bus stops adjacent to the TIC. (See Powys Travel Guide, available free from TICs in Powys, for general information).

1 Starting from the Lakeside tourist facilities, follow the pavement around the lake in a clockwise direction, past a kissing gate and large gate on the left, until reaching the picnic area on the right. Cross the road with care and join the waymarked footpath opposite. Follow the path, which is at first gravelled, up through trees to reach the junction with another path. Continue AHEAD and exit the woodland via a footgate. Turn RIGHT and follow the path towards the old parish church (*originally 13th century, rebuilt in 1894*) visible ahead. Go through a gate and across the road to reach the church. Go through a wooden gate to the left side of the church grounds and cross to the footgate opposite. Turn RIGHT and follow the line of the wall around the church grounds till reaching the corner of the field. Pass through a gate and descend a flight of steps to a track.

2 Turn LEFT and follow the track to and through a gate into upland sheep pastures. Continue round to the right. After the next gateway, take the left fork in the track, following a fence to your left. When the fence turns uphill, continue AHEAD on a track that heads slightly to the left, climbing steadily

between areas of bracken. Pass through a gate and continue along the track, passing between two sheep feeders. Just before reaching a next gate, bear LEFT (by a waymark post) and head uphill towards another stile in the fence line ahead. Go straight across the field to another stile and follow the path through bracken for a short way, going straight AHEAD at the first waymark post and passing through a gate on the right. Head HALF LEFT for a few yards and then take the path that bends to the right, just before the second waymark post. Follow the path down the slope, keeping the fence line to your left. Turn LEFT at the third waymark post, still keeping the fence line to your left and continue until reaching a stile in the fence. Cross and turn RIGHT to follow a track for a few yards to a stile giving onto a narrow lane.

3 Turn RIGHT in the lane and bead down hill and round a bend to the left. (This lane gives access to and from the Llandrindod Wells to Builth Wells bus route, on the main road adjacent to Howey village). When the lane bends to the right, turn LEFT into the waymarked driveway leading to Acorn Court and Three Wells B&Bs. Shortly after passing the turning for Acorn Court, cross the stile on the right. Go straight across the field to a footbridge and stile. Cross the next field to another stile, then cut across the corner of a third field to reach a footbridge and stile to the right. Cross the fourth field, heading for a stile to the right of a gate. Go straight AHEAD along a track, passing through two gates in quick succession. Shortly thereafter, take the left fork in the track, passing another gate into a wooded area. Continue along the track for a short way, until reaching a stile in the fence on the right. Cross and head HALF LEFT up the bank, passing an old farm building. Turn LEFT on the access track and walk up to the junction with the road. (The road also provides access to and from the Llandrindod Wells to Builth Wells bus route, as above).

4 Turn LEFT on the road (which follows the course of an old Drover's Route to Kington in England) and follow this for about three-quarters of a mile, passing a side road and a driveway to the right. Take the third turning to the right, by a post box. Follow the scenic lane for about one mile, until the lane bends to the right. Go STRAIGHT AHEAD through the waymarked field gate and follow the track, passing a ruined cottage (Tynlliddiart) on the left, to reach a second gate giving access onto the Carneddau hills. On reaching the open land, turn LEFT and ascend the hill until above the bracken line. Bear RIGHT at this point and follow the high ground towards the south (there are good views on this stretch also). Look for and head towards a fence and old wall to the right. Follow the track running to the left of this boundary. The track runs roughly parallel the fence for some way and then skirts around the shoulders of the hills at the southern end of the Carneddau. *The two southernmost hills are the sites of hillforts – Caer Fawr being near the walking route and Caer Einon off to the left.* After about two miles, cross a small stream and take the broader track that bends slightly to the left. Continue on this track, now passing above farmland below you to the left. Pass through a footgate

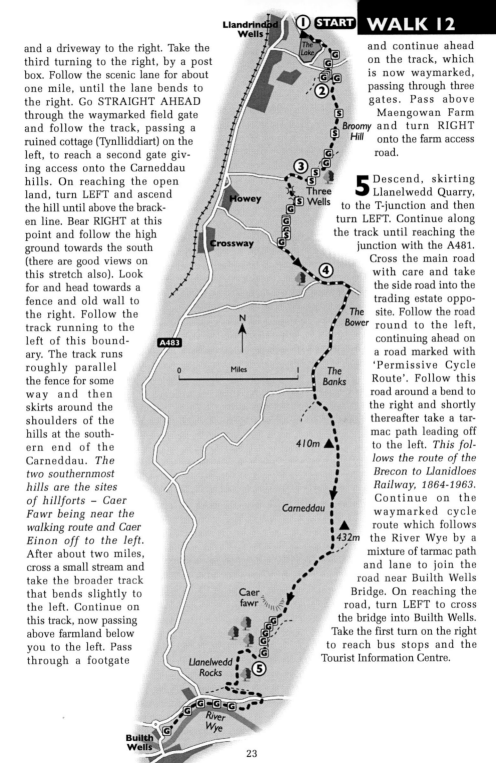

and continue ahead on the track, which is now waymarked, passing through three gates. Pass above Maengowan Farm and turn RIGHT onto the farm access road.

5 Descend, skirting Llanelwedd Quarry, to the T-junction and then turn LEFT. Continue along the track until reaching the junction with the A481. Cross the main road with care and take the side road into the trading estate opposite. Follow the road round to the left, continuing ahead on a road marked with 'Permissive Cycle Route'. Follow this road around a bend to the right and shortly thereafter take a tarmac path leading off to the left. *This follows the route of the Brecon to Llanidloes Railway, 1864-1963.* Continue on the waymarked cycle route which follows the River Wye by a mixture of tarmac path and lane to join the road near Builth Wells Bridge. On reaching the road, turn LEFT to cross the bridge into Builth Wells. Take the first turn on the right to reach bus stops and the Tourist Information Centre.

WYE VALLEY CIRCULAR, BUILTH WELLS

DESCRIPTION A choice of either 5 or 8¾ miles. The outward route (of about 5 miles) follows a scenic riverside section of the Wye Valley Walk and then crosses adjacent countryside, by bridlepath and lane, to Cilmeri. There is the option of a pub lunch and a visit to a local historical site. The return route (of about 3¾ miles) is via footpath, lane and bridlepath. Allow about 3 or 5 hours for the walk.

START Tourist Information Centre, The Groe, Builth Wells. SO 042512.

PUBLIC TRANSPORT Builth Wells is on the bus route from a number of local towns, including the TrawsCambria Brecon/Newtown service. Buses stop outside and opposite the Tourist Information Centre. Cilmeri is a request stop on the Heart of Wales line. A post bus no longer covers this route but there is a Crossgates service (01597 852000) between Builth Road railway station and The Groe. (See Powys Travel Guide, available free from Tourist Information Centres in Powys, for further details,). The station can be found by following the lane adjacent to the Prince Llewelyn pub/restaurant. (Cilmeri is a request stop, so signal as for a bus).

I **Builth Wells to Cilmeri** (*5 miles*). From The Groe/Tourist Information Centre, follow the tarmac path alongside the River Wye. Turn LEFT at the junction with the River Irfon to follow the path over a footbridge, and then bear RIGHT to a kissing gate. Follow the path back to the River Wye and continue AHEAD through fields, woodland (passing under the Heart of Wales railway bridge) and back to fields, passing through five footgates and over seven stiles (the County Council seem to be in the process of replacing stiles with footgates on this section of the National Trail).

2 On reaching a farm access track with a bridlepath sign, after about two miles, turn LEFT away from the river. Follow the access track past a pond on the right and Dolyrerw farm on the left. Shortly after passing the farm, take an unmarked path on the right, leading towards Coed Dolyrerw wood. Just before reaching the wood, turn LEFT and follow a waymarked path.

3 Follow the path through a short section of bracken (quite often flattened down by previous users) and continue along the right hand side of a small valley. When the path levels off, cross another section of bracken (again this may be flattened), keeping close to the hedgeline on the right. Eventually, pass through a gate, go AHEAD between trees and pass through a second gate to a road.

4 Cross the road, aiming for the lane slightly to the right. Follow this down to the right of Rhosferig-Fawr farmhouse and go through a gate across the track. Continue down, turning RIGHT on reaching a railway bridge on the left. Pass through another farmyard, head LEFT over a river bridge and turn RIGHT to head up a lane. At the junction with the main road, turn RIGHT and follow the road past the Prince Llewelyn pub/restaurant to reach the monument to Prince Llewelyn on the left. There is also a well at this site, located down steps in the far right corner of the monument area. *Llywelyn ap Gruffydd, the last native Prince of Wales, was killed in battle at Cilmeri on 11th December 1282.*

5 **Cilmeri to Builth Wells** (*3¾ miles*). Return along the road, until reaching the 'Old Post Office' on the left. Follow the footpath sign along the driveway and over a stile on the right. Head DIAGONALLY across the field, aiming slightly to the left of the telegraph pole. Follow marker posts through a short section of woodland and then cross a field to access the churchyard via a stile.

Cilmery

station

8 Follow the left-hand boundary of the field and cross a new driveway, by means of gates. Head to the far right corner of the next field, pass through a narrow band of conifers and cross a stile. Head SLIGHTLY TO THE RIGHT across the next field and follow a track and stiles through a wooded area – skirting the edge of Park Wells house on the left. On reaching a small field, continue along the right hand side of this, until reaching a stile on the right, leading into woodland.

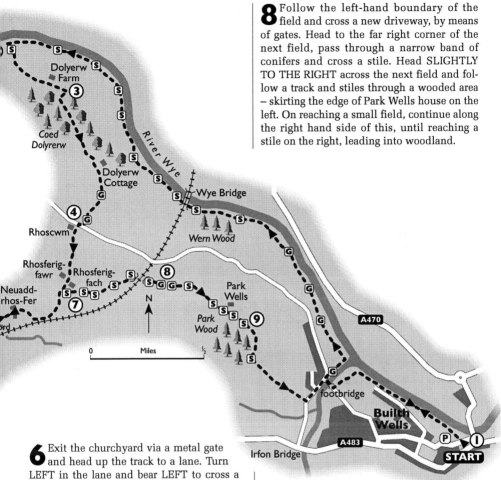

6 Exit the churchyard via a metal gate and head up the track to a lane. Turn LEFT in the lane and bear LEFT to cross a river bridge. Turn RIGHT to follow the track through Neuadd-rhos-Fer farmyard and up towards Rhosferig-fawr farm. Just after passing through a gate below the second farm, take a stile to the right.

7 Head LEFT, past an unmarked finger post, to a stile next to a watering trough. Head for a gate directly in front, passing to the right of Rhosferig-Fach house. After a few yards, cross a stile on the right. Head down the field and to the left to access a stile giving onto the railway line. Descend, using alternating steps and walkways and cross the line with care. Head up the opposite bank to another stile.

9 Turn LEFT on the path through the woodland and continue until reaching a stile on the left leading on to the golf course. Follow the track across the golf course (keeping an eye out for stray golf balls) to the road. Head LEFT along the road until reaching the footbridge crossed on the way out from Builth Wells. Cross and turn LEFT to follow the tarmac riverside path back to The Groe/Tourist Information Centre.

WYE, IRFON & GARTH, BUILTH WELLS

DESCRIPTION A 6½ mile walk along the scenic Wye and Irfon rivers, followed by a quiet footpath, lane and road route to Garth, a local viewpoint. The route then follows the Wye Valley Walk back to Builth Wells, passing the site of Builth Castle on the way. Allow about 3½ hours.
START Tourist Information Centre, The Groe, Builth Wells. SO 042512.
PUBLIC TRANSPORT Bus stops adjacent to/opposite the Tourist Information Centre (See Powys Travel Guide, available from Tourist Information Centres, for details).

I From the Tourist Information Centre, follow the Wye Valley Walk along the scenic riverside path for about half a mile. On reaching the junction with the River Irfon, follow the tarmac path around to the left. Leave the Wye Valley Walk where it crosses a footbridge on the right. Continue AHEAD along a footpath that follows the River Irfon. Climb up the steps at the side of the Irfon Bridge and go through a footgate. Cross the main road (A483) with care and enter Irfon Bridge Road opposite. Follow the road along the side of the Irfon. The footpaths on the other side of the river are part of the grounds of Caer Beris Hotel. When the road bends to the left, cross the stile on the right. Continue along the Irfon – *less placid than the Wye and now showing 'white water'*. On reaching a lane, turn LEFT and continue to a junction with a minor road.

2 Cross the road and take the waymarked stile slightly to the right. Head up the left hand side of the field, pass through a gate and continue along the left hand side of the next field. On coming to a fence, pass through a gate on the left and continue along the line of the old track. At the end of the track, cross stile on the right. Head up the left side of the field and go LEFT through a gate. Follow right hand side of field and then aim HALF LEFT to reach the lower of two gates. Continue AHEAD to the next gate. Maintain direction over two stiles. Head HALF LEFT to gate, cross small stream and continue AHEAD alongside hedge to reach a gate onto a lane.

3 Follow the lane to the left. Pass the turning on the left, for Erwhelm. At the junction, turn LEFT onto the B4520. Turn RIGHT at the next junction and then LEFT at a third junction. Pass the turning, on the right, for Maes-y-cwm. At the next junction, cross the waymarked stile ahead. Follow the gradual ascent, through two footgates to the viewpoint at the trig point on Garth – *this gives excellent views of the Wye Valley, Builth Wells and the southern end of the Carneddau*. When ready, retrace the route back to the road and turn RIGHT. Follow the road towards Builth Wells.

4 On reaching a T-junction within the town, turn RIGHT and then follow the road around to the left. *A footpath sign on the left indicates the entrance to Builth Castle site, which provides additional views over the town.* The main route leads to the main road, turns left and – when getting to the beginning of the shops – crosses the road and takes the first turn to the left to return to The Groe.

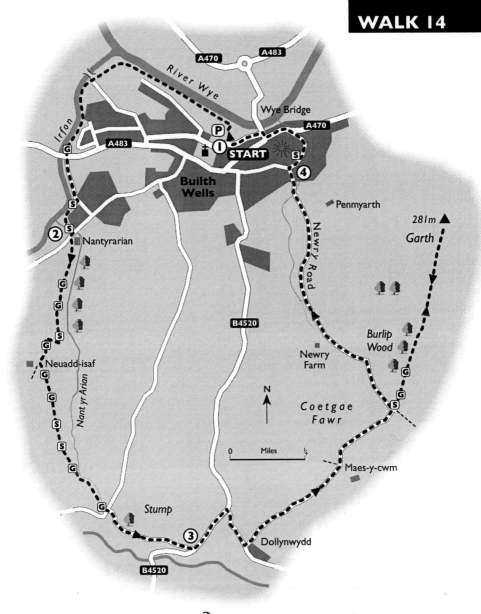

Builth Wells

START

Wye Bridge

Penmyarth

281m Garth

Newry Road

Nantyrarian

Neuadd-isaf

Nant yr Arian

Burlip Wood

Newry Farm

Coetgae Fawr

N

0 Miles ¼

Maes-y-cwm

Stump

Dollynwydd

B4520

Wye Bridge at Builth Wells

CORS Y LLYN National Nature Reserve

DESCRIPTION A 3 mile walk, plus a boardwalk route through a National Nature Reserve. This walk follows a bridlepath across fields (giving excellent views of farmland and hills around) and then a scenic lane, before joining a footpath across fields, some of which are part the Nature Reserve. The route then follows a boardwalk across Cors y Llyn (a lake that has been overgrown by floating vegetation) where Sir David Attenborough once filmed. Allow about 2 hours for the walk.

START This walk can be started at either the bus stop near Caerwnon Caravan Park (SO 028545) or at the Parking Area near the entrance to Cors y Llyn (SO 016556). If starting from the former, begin following the directions at point **2** below and use point **1** as the final part of the walk.

PUBLIC TRANSPORT Caerwnon Caravan Park (entrance) is on the Crossgates bus route to and from Builth Wells (01597 852000).

1 Continue along the lane (turn LEFT into the lane if walking to and from the bus stop at Caerwnon Park) and turn LEFT through a gate, on reaching a farm building on the left. Follow an enclosed track through two gates. Continue AHEAD along the right hand side of the next three fields, connected by gates. Follow the right hand side of the next field (the track is becoming increasingly clear to follow at this point) and exit via a gate onto a lane. Turn LEFT and follow the lane to the bus stop by Caerwnon Park. (*The bridlepath starting adjacent to the bus stop leads only to the River Wye – the lane from Glan-Gwy to Builth Road is not a public right of way*).

2 Continue along the lane past the bus stop for a short way (if starting from Caerwnon, retrace the route of the bus for a short way), until reaching a footpath sign on the left. Cross into a small area of woodland. Go HALF LEFT through the trees and skirt around the right side of fencing ahead. Aim HALF LEFT across the field, crossing a small stream, to reach a waymarked stile. Continue HALF LEFT, aiming to the left of farm buildings visible ahead, to reach a waymarked stile in the hedge on the left. Continue HALF RIGHT across the field to reach a further stile. Continue HALF RIGHT across a large field to reach a gate onto a track. Turn LEFT and cross a waymarked stile to the right of a gate.

3 Continue AHEAD, passing through an open gateway and along the right hand side of the next field. Pass through trees and across an area of cleared land to a stile. (The route now leads through fields that are part of the National Nature Reserve). Continue AHEAD through a waymarked gateway, going HALF LEFT on reaching a waymark sign on the fence to the left. Pass through a gate and turn RIGHT, to reach a further gate. Bear HALF RIGHT to reach the entrance to Cors y Llyn.

4 Enter the national nature reserve. *IT IS IMPORTANT TO KEEP TO THE BOARDWALK AT ALL TIMES – NOTE SAFETY NOTICE AT THE ENTRANCE.* Follow the boardwalk to the barrier and return by same route. On leaving the reserve, follow the waymarks around the edge of the field ahead. Pass through a footgate and along the left hand side of a field to another footgate onto a lane.

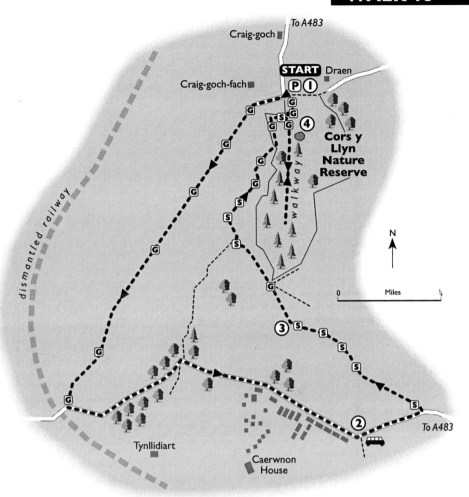

To A483
Craig-goch
START Draen
Craig-goch-fach
(4)
**Cors y
Llyn
Nature
Reserve**
walkway
N
Miles 0 ¼
(3)
(2)
To A483
Tynllidiart
dismantled railway
Caerwnon
House

Cors y Llyn

LLANDRINDOD WELLS TO NEWBRIDGE-ON-WYE

DESCRIPTION A 5½ mile walk, mostly along footpaths and quiet lanes. This route provides views of countryside and surrounding hills, as well as the opportunity to visit a local wetland nature reserve. There is a bus access point about half way through the walk as well as in Newbridge-on-Wye. There is the option of a pub lunch in Newbridge. Allow up to 3 hours.
START Llandrindod Wells Lake.
SO 063606.
PUBLIC TRANSPORT Llandrindod Wells is on the Heart of Wales Railway Line and has several bus services, including the TrawsCambria Brecon-Newtown. Newbridge-on-Wye is on the bus route to and from Llandrindod Wells, as well as other local towns (See Powys Travel Guide, available free from Tourist Information Centres in Powys, for general information).

1 Starting from the Lakeside tourist facilities, follow the pavement around the lake in a clockwise direction until reaching the picnic area on the right. Cross the road with care and join the waymarked footpath opposite. Follow the path, which is at first gravelled, up through trees to reach the junction with another path. Cross the second path and exit the woodland via a footgate. Turn RIGHT and follow the path towards the old parish church visible ahead. Go through a gate and cross the road to reach the old parish church – *originally 13th Century, rebuilt in 1894.* Go through a wooden gate to the left side of the church grounds and cross to the footgate opposite.

2 Turn RIGHT and follow the line of the wall around the church grounds till reaching the corner of the field. Pass through a gate and descend a flight of steps to a track. Turn RIGHT and follow the track for a short

way. On reaching a waymark post on the right, bear LEFT up the bank towards a way-marked stile. Cross and bear HALF RIGHT, following the line of the trees and passing to the left of a house to reach another track. Turn LEFT on the track.

3 Continue AHEAD on the track (the entrance to Pentrosfa Mire Nature Reserve is on the right – *the reserve can be visited via a stile from this section of the walk* – after which return to the main route and turn RIGHT). Continue AHEAD through a waymarked gate and follow the left hand boundary of the next two fields. Towards the end of the second field, bear HALF RIGHT to reach a stile.

4 Cross and continue HALF RIGHT across the next field. Turn RIGHT to walk between hedges for a short way, then cross a stile on the left. Continue along the right hand side of the next field to a further stile. Cross and continue for a short way to a stile on the right. Cross and head for the far left corner of the next field. Cross a stile into a

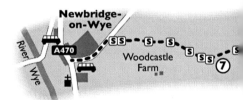

clump of trees. Pass through these and continue HALF LEFT on a clear path – *passing Caer Du earthworks on the left* – to reach a kissing gate onto an enclosed track.

5 Follow the track to the junction with a minor road. Turn RIGHT and then LEFT and follow the road through Howey village. (The mid-walk bus access point can be reached by turning RIGHT just after the Post Office – buses to Builth Wells stop just to the right of the junction. For buses to Llandrindod, use the lay-by opposite). After passing the Post Office, continue AHEAD between the Telephone Box and the Village Hall. At the end of this road, follow the path down to the pavement and head LEFT along the main road to the staggered crossroads. Cross the road with care and take the right turn, signposted for Newbridge-on-Wye and Disserth. Follow this quiet road for about one mile to reach Disserth – *there are good views of the church on the way down.*

6 Cross the bridge – *good views of the Ithon at this point* – then turn LEFT onto a footpath. Follow the left boundary of the field over a footbridge, into another section of woodland. Climb the wooden steps up the bank (this is steep but not very long) and continue through the woodland to a stile. Cross the field beyond, then cross a track by means of stiles. Turn RIGHT, keeping close the fence on the right. On reaching a waymark arrow, on the remains of a tree, head along the right hand side of the field (passing another waymark arrow on the remains of a tree stump to the right of a gate).

7 Cross a stile to the right of a gate and continue along the right hand side of the next field, Cross a stile and then turn RIGHT to cross a second stile. Aim slightly to the left when crossing the next two fields, connected by stiles, passing through a line of trees between these. Head along the left side of the next field to a stile. Follow the path along the old boundary of the field to reach a stile just to the left of a telegraph pole, then cross the final field to a stile giving onto a road. Turn LEFT and follow the pavement into Newbridge-on-Wye.

AROUND NEWBRIDGE-ON-WYE

DESCRIPTION A pleasant walk of some 4¼ miles around the village of Newbridge-on-Wye. This includes riverside, field and woodland sections, with good views of the hills around. Pub lunches are available in the village. Allow about 2½ hours for the walk.
START The Village Green, Newbridge-on-Wye. SO 016583.
PUBLIC TRANSPORT Newbridge-on-Wye is on bus routes to and from other towns in the area, including Llandrindod Wells.

1 From the Village Green – *note the statue of a Drover and the willow seat* – head along the B4358 towards Llandrindod Wells for just under a quarter of a mile. Cross a stile on the left onto a waymarked footpath leading down to the right of the field to a footbridge. Cross and continue AHEAD, along the bank and keeping the hedgeline to the right. Cross a stile into a lane and turn LEFT.

2 On reaching the road, cross to a side road slightly to the left, which leads to the Rhayader-Beulah road. Cross the road with care and follow the footpath sign down a no through road ahead. Go through the gate at the bottom and continue AHEAD to the river. Turn RIGHT and follow the river until reaching the remains of a railway bridge. When ready, retrace your steps to the Rhayader-Beulah road.

3 Turn RIGHT and follow the road down to the bridge, for a view of the River Wye and of Llysdinam and its surrounding parkland (*Llysdinam is a member of the National Gardens Scheme – www.ngs.org.uk*) When ready, retrace your steps up to the side road and back to the village street. Turn RIGHT and follow the village street past the Village Green and the church – *built in 1883 by S.W. Williams for the Venables family of Llysdinam.*

4 On approaching the outskirts of the village, turn RIGHT onto a bridlepath (the sign may be part hidden in a hedge on the right) leading through a gate into a wooded strip – *part of which is the course of the old railway line.* The bridlepath appears to be the only right of way leading into this area, but there are well-established paths within it, including a section overlooking the Wye. When ready, return to the village street and retrace your steps to the church.

5 Cross the road and follow a footpath sign opposite. Go past the school and follow the path between fences, until coming to a gate into a field. Continue AHEAD, keeping to the left of a hedge to reach a stile. Follow the footpath along the right hand boundary of the field, joining another footpath coming from the left. *There are good views of the hills towards Rhayader from this point.* Continue to follow the old boundary line of the field until reaching a stile on the right, near a telegraph pole. Cross a further small field to a final stile and turn LEFT to follow the pavement back to the Village Green.

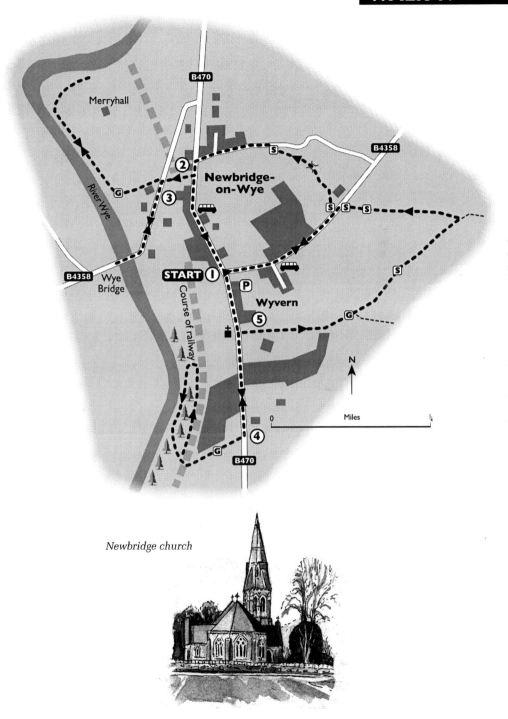

Merryhall

B470

River Wye

B4358

②

Newbridge-on-Wye

G

③

S

S S S

S

B4358
Wye
Bridge

START ①

P

Wyvern

⑤

G

S

Course of railway

N

0   Miles   ¼

G

B470

④

Newbridge church

WYE VALLEY WALK, CWM CLYD & TY-LINK

DESCRIPTION A 9 mile walk, following the Wye Valley Walk south across farmland from Newbridge-on-Wye, before joining a lane and bridlepath route to Cwm Clyd. From here, the route passes by lanes and bridlepaths through traditional Welsh farming country, where there are more tracks and rights off way than roads, plus a range of great views. Allow about 5 hours for the walk

START The Village Green, Newbridge-on-Wye. SO 016583.

PUBLIC TRANSPORT Newbridge-on-Wye is on a number of local bus routes (See Powys Travel Guide, available free from Tourist Information Centres in Powys, for general information)

I From the Village Green, head RIGHT through the village. Pass the Golden Lion and turn LEFT into a side road that leads to the Rhayader to Beulah road. Turn LEFT and follow the main road over the Wye Bridge. Continue AHEAD up a hill section and turn LEFT through a gate (Wye Valley Walk waymark post here). Follow the Wye Valley Walk through Estyn Pitch Wood, over a stile and up the left hand side of the field to another stile. Follow the right boundary of the next two fields, passing through an open gateway and then head towards a waymark post in the far left corner of the next field.

2 Descend the bank to a stile and footbridge. Continue AHEAD over the next two stiles (with new hedge on the right for part of the way). Go through trees and cross stile in far right corner of field. Head HALF LEFT to a waymark post in a hedge gap. Pass through and follow left boundary of field to stile on left. Cross and follow right hand side of field to stile onto lane. Turn RIGHT and follow lane to crossroads. Turn RIGHT and follow lane past two properties and a further

access track on the left. Ignore the footpath sign leading into the wood on the left, and continue AHEAD to a bridlepath waymark post on the left.

3 Turn LEFT and go through a footgate into the wood. Follow the course of an old track along the right hand boundary of the wood to a further footgate. Continue AHEAD over some seven fields, connected by waymarked footgates and gates, following the clear line of the old track as it follows field boundaries. Eventually, pass through a gate onto the main Rhayader to Beulah road. Cross the main road with care and turn LEFT.

4 Pass the roadside church and turn RIGHT into a lane that leads through a traditional Welsh farming valley. At the end of the lane, continue AHEAD on a broad track into a forested area. On reaching cottage on the left and gate into National Trust land, turn RIGHT through a gate and follow a broad track over a bridge and towards a house (there has been forestry clearance work carried out here, but a clear track has been left). Just before the house, bear LEFT and continue along through a forested area.

5 On leaving the forestry area, continue AHEAD, into a scenic area of farmland and hill views. At the junction of tracks, continue AHEAD and cross the cattle grid. At the next junction, bear RIGHT. Cross the cattle grid to join the tarmaced lane. Descend towards Nantgwyn and turn LEFT at the T-junction. Descend past Pentre Farm. After a few yards, when the road bends to the left, take the track on the right. Pass through a gate and over a cattle grid. Follow the track around to the left. At a fork in the track, continue LEFT on the main route. Pass through a gate and continue along the right hand side of the field to another gate. Pass through and follow the course of an old track down the left hand side of the field to the next gate. Head HALF RIGHT to a footbridge. Cross and continue to Penyrhiw, turning LEFT on the track.

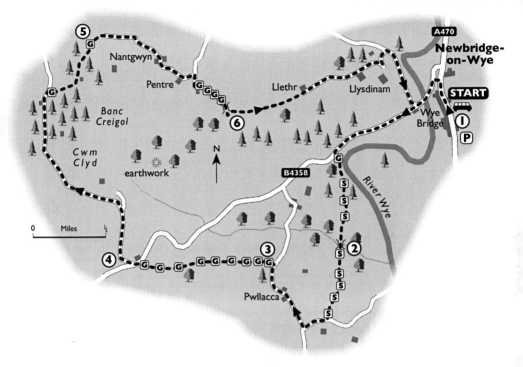

6 Head RIGHT at the junction of tracks. Follow the track over a further two cattle grids to meet the end of a lane. Follow the scenic lane for about half a mile to a T-junction (passing Cardiff University, School of Biosciences, Field Centre near Llysdinam Lodge). Turn RIGHT and follow the road down to the junction with the main road. Turn LEFT and cross the Wye Bridge. Continue along past the chapel and then turn RIGHT into a side road on the right. Turn RIGHT at the junction with the village street to return to Newbridge-on-Wye.

WALK 19

ABERGWESYN COMMON & WYE VALLEY

DESCRIPTION A 9 mile walk following a quiet road (providing a view of Llysdinam house) and lane through parkland, fields and woods to open access land owned by the National Trust. It crosses a section of the open land, providing excellent views of the hills and valleys around, before descending to join the Wye Valley Walk and follow bridlepath, lane and footpaths back to the minor road near Llysdinam and then back to Newbridge-on-Wye. Allow about 5 hours for the walk.

START The Village Green, Newbridge-on-Wye. SO 016583.

PUBLIC TRANSPORT Newbridge-on-Wye is on a number of local bus routes (See Powys Travel Guide, available free from Tourist Information Centres in Powys, for general information)

1 From the Village Green, head RIGHT into Newbridge-on-Wye. Continue past the Golden Lion and turn LEFT into a side road that leads to the Rhayader to Beulah road. Cross the main road with care and head LEFT along the pavement to cross the Wye Bridge. Turn RIGHT into a side road just after the bridge.

2 Follow the minor road, past Llysdinam on the left, as it climbs gradually through parkland, then a mixture of fields and woods until reaching views of the surrounding hills. On reaching a crossroads, where the National Cycleway turns right, continue AHEAD on the lane. Pass Blaenglynolwyn farm and continue AHEAD on the bridlepath, which leads through a gate onto open access land owned by the National Trust.

3 On coming to a junction of tracks, take the track on the right. Follow the fence line on the right, until this veers right, and then continue STRAIGHT AHEAD across open ground for about three-quarters of a mile until coming in sight of a valley to the left. Cross towards the left side of the hill and gradually descend towards a path running along the lower slopes, just above the fields (there is more than one clear route through the bracken on this slope). Continue to the RIGHT along this path, to join a bridlepath section of the Wye Valley Walk, at the start of a wooded area.

4 Turn RIGHT on the Wye Valley Walk, keeping an eye out for the view of Doldowlod House (once owned by the inventor James Watt) through a gap in the trees to the left. Follow the track to the end of the National Trust land and then through farmland to reach a lane. Turn RIGHT and follow the winding lane gradually uphill until reaching a Wye Valley Walk waymark post and stile (at a point where the lane bends to the right).

5 Head along the left side of the field, cross a footbridge and stile and then head RIGHT to a second footbridge and steps. Climb the bank to a waymark post, turn LEFT to follow the stream and then head SLIGHTLY TO THE RIGHT to cross a stile. Continue AHEAD, keeping to the right of a fence. Cross another footbridge and take the left hand stile. Go along the right hand side of the field, cross a further footbridge and follow a short length of track to a stile. Turn LEFT and follow the track as far as the first house, then head RIGHT and across the field (keeping close to left boundary). Cross the left side of the next three fields, then cut across the middle of a further field to footbridges. Head along the right hand side of the final two fields to reach the minor road near Llysdinam. Turn LEFT, follow the road back to the Rhayader-Beulah road and retrace your steps to Newbridge-on-Wye.

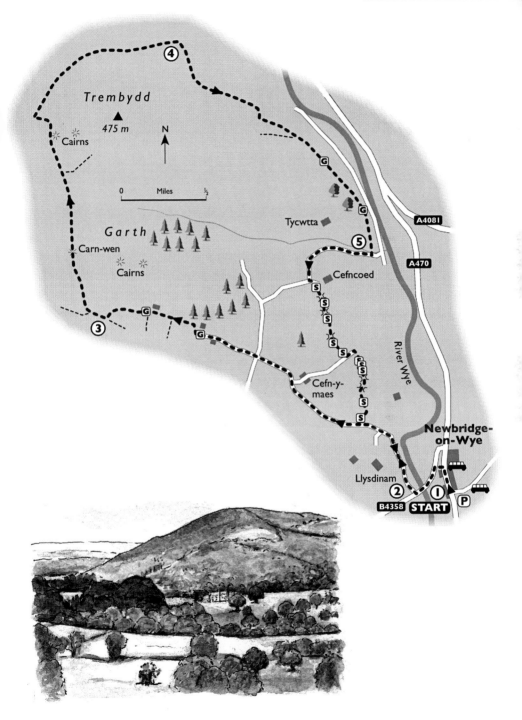

WALK 20
ABERGWESYN COMMON

DESCRIPTION A 7½ mile walk starting from the village of Llanwrthl, this route heads up a scenic valley before crossing open access hills with excellent views over the Elan Valley and following a waterside route to the Elan Valley Visitor Centre/Elan Village. Allow about 4¼ hours for the walk.

START Llanwrthl Village near Rhayader. SN 976637.

PUBLIC TRANSPORT *Llanwrthl* – Bus services run between Llandrindod Wells, Builth Wells and Rhayader. Some buses enter Llanwrthl village, others stop on the nearby main road. *Elan Valley* – the weekday Post Bus calls at the Elan Valley Visitor Centre, *between April and October*, on route for Rhayader. This service goes on to Llanwrthl after a scenic detour. (See Powys Travel Guide, available free from TICs in Powys, for general information).

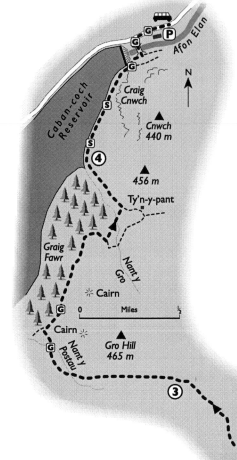

1 Follow the scenic lane running to the right of the church. At the next junction, take the left fork. Continue along the scenic lane for about two miles. At the end of the lane, continue AHEAD on the track, passing a National Trust Marker for Abergwesyn Common. Continue on the track for about ¼ mile and then bear RIGHT on a track, aiming for the paths now visible running up the hill to the right. *This section provides views of the Cwm Chwefri and hills to the south and east.*

2 Aim for the left hand path that heads diagonally around the shoulder of the hill, rather than the steeper, vertical ascents. Continue AHEAD, keeping to the left of a series of rock outcroppings. At the end of the outcroppings, start to descend gradually towards the forestry plantation ahead. *The other hills around Caban-Coch are also visible from this point.*

3 Descend gradually from this point, aiming in a direction which is generally HALF LEFT, passing to the left of Gro Hill. Pass through a gate and on reaching the conifer plantation, turn RIGHT through a gate and follow the clear path. The circle of trees visible to the right indicates the location of the ruined cottage. On reaching the end of the forestry plantation turn LEFT and follow the path, which is steep in places, down towards the reservoir.

4 At the bottom of the descent, turn RIGHT and follow the waymarked path towards the Elan Valley Visitor Centre, crossing two stiles on this section of the route. At the end of the waterside section, follow the path for a

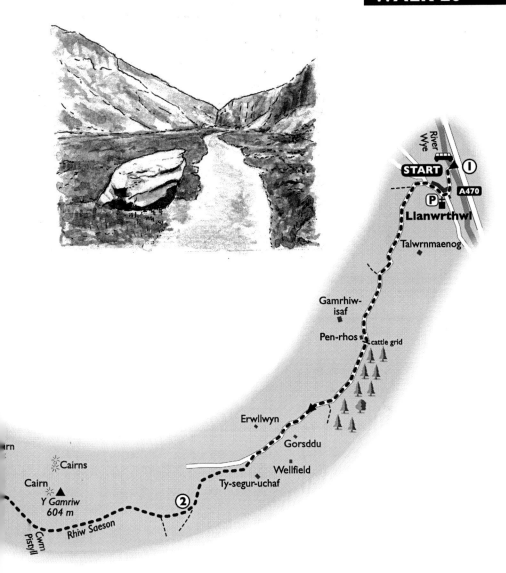

little way further – *passing a viewpoint over the reservoir and dam on the left* – and then pass through a footgate on the left. Descend the steps and pass to the left of the pumping house, across the bridge and round the left side of the next pumping house. Follow the track to the right, through a footgate and ahead to the Visitor Centre.

PRONUNCIATION

These basic points should help non-Welsh speakers

Welsh	English equivalent
c	always hard, as in cat
ch	as on the Scottish word loch
dd	as th in then
f	as in of
ff	as in off
g	always hard as in got
ll	no real equivalent. It is like 'th' in then, but with an 'L' sound added to it, giving 'thlan' for the pronunciation of the Welsh 'Llan'.

In Welsh the accent usually falls on the last-but-one syllable of a word.

KEY TO THE MAPS

- —— Main road
- —— Minor road
- ●▶ Walk route and direction
- ① Walk instruction
- - - - Path
- ∿ River/stream
- Ⓖ Gate
- Ⓢ Stile
- △ Summit
- ♣ Woods
- 🍺 Pub
- Ⓟ Parking
- 🚌 Bus service

THE COUNTRYSIDE CODE

- Be safe – plan ahead and follow any signs
- Leave gates and property as you find them
- Protect plants and animals, and take your litter home
- Keep dogs under close control
- Consider other people

The CRoW Act 2000, implemented throughout Wales in May 2005, introduced new legal rights of access for walkers to designated open country, predominantly mountain, moor, heath or down, plus all registered common land. This access can be subject to restrictions and closure for land management or safety reasons for up to 28 days a year. The following web site operated by Countryside Council for Wales will provide updated information on any closures.
www.ccw.gov.uk/countrysideaccesswales

Published by
Kittiwake
3 Glantwymyn Village Workshops, Glantwymyn, Machynlleth, Montgomeryshire SY20 8LY

© Text & map research: Jane Griffiths 2007
© Maps & illustrations: Kittiwake 2007
Drawings by Morag Perrott

Cover photos: *Main* – Cefnllys from Shaky Bridge.
Inset – St Michael's Church, Cefnllys. David Perrott

Printed by MWL, Pontypool.

ISBN: **978 1 902302 51 5**